Ghost Po

Compiled by John Foster

OXFORD

Oxford University Press, Great Clarendon Street, Oxford
OX2 6DP

Oxford   New York
Athens   Auckland   Bangkok   Bogota   Bombay
Buenos Aires   Calcutta   Cape Town   Dar es Salaam
Delhi   Florence   Hong Kong   Istanbul   Karachi
Kuala Lumpur   Madras   Madrid   Melbourne
Mexico City   Nairobi   Paris   Singapore
Taipei   Tokyo   Toronto

and associated companies in
Berlin   Ibadan

Oxford is a trade mark of Oxford University Press

© Oxford University Press 1991
Published 1992
Reprinted 1992, 1993, 1995, 1996, 1997
ISBN 0 19 916429 0
Printed in Hong Kong

A CIP catalogue record for this book is available from the British
Library.

Acknowledgements
The Editor and Publisher wish to thank the following who have
kindly given permission for the use of copyright materials:

Ann Bonner for 'The Night Visitor' ©1990 Ann Bonner; John Foster
for 'What's that?', 'The Shadow Man', 'The Haunted House' and
'Who's Afraid?' all ©1990 John Foster; James Kirkup for 'The house
at night' ©1990 James Kirkup; Lutterworth Press and Richard
Edwards for 'The Boastful Ghost' from Whispers from a Wardrobe;
Judith Nicholls for 'Ghostly Lessons' ©1990 Judith Nicholls.

Although every effort has been made to contact the owners of
copyright material, a few have been impossible to trace, but if they
contact the Publisher correct acknowledgement will be made in
future editions.

Illustrations by
Rowan Barnes-Murphy, Alan Marks, Jan Lewis, Dominic Mansell,
Frances Cony.

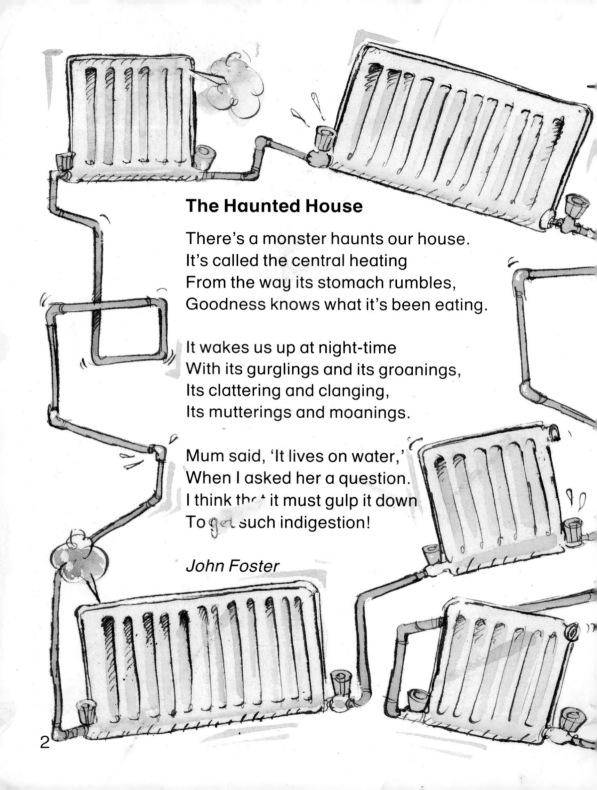

The Haunted House

There's a monster haunts our house.
It's called the central heating
From the way its stomach rumbles,
Goodness knows what it's been eating.

It wakes us up at night-time
With its gurglings and its groanings,
Its clattering and clanging,
Its mutterings and moanings.

Mum said, 'It lives on water,'
When I asked her a question.
I think that it must gulp it down
To get such indigestion!

John Foster

What's that?

What's that rustling at the window?
Only the curtain flapping in the breeze.

What's that groaning in the garden?
Only the branches swaying in the trees.

What's that rattling at the front door?
Only the wind in the letter-box flap.

What's that drumming in the bathroom?
Only the dripping of the leaking tap.

What's that hissing in the front room?
Only the gas as it burns in the fire.

What's that murmur in the kitchen?
Only the whirring of the tumble drier.

What's that shadow lurking
   in the corner beside the door?
It's only your clothes where you left them
   lying on the bedroom floor.

John Foster

The Night Visitor

Some
THING
went
bump
in the
night.

THUMP
in the
night.
Gave
me a
fright.

A shadow
moved
on the
wall.
Long-
legged
and
terribly
tall.

A ghoulie?
Or
ghostie
in white?
A trick
of the
light?

No.
Nothing
went
bump
but that
BEASTLY

lump
of a
cat.
Asleep!
On my
bed.

She
made me
jump
last night.

Ann Bonner

The Shadow Man

At night-time
As I climb the stair
I tell myself
There's nobody there.

But what if there is?
What if he's there −
The Shadow Man
At the top of the stair?

What if he's lurking
There in the gloom
Of the landing
Right outside my room?

The Shadow Man
Who's so hard to see
What if he's up there
Waiting for me?

At night-time
As I climb the stair
I tell myself
There's nobody there.

John Foster

The house at night

When it grows dark
We go to our beds,
And nothing exists
But the dreams in our heads.

Yet while we're asleep
The house soon awakes:
It rustles and rattles
And shudders and shakes!

The drainpipes gurgle,
The windowpanes sigh,
The floors toss and turn
And the chimneypots cry.

The house sounds as if
It's taking a break,
With time off from *us*
And the racket we make.

So it stretches its arms
And relaxes a while.
And on its old face
There's a sly little smile.

It flings up its tiles
And lets down its hair,
Then does a wild tap-dance
Up and down stair.

11

And sometimes if you
Wake up in the night
You can catch it at play,
And it gives you a fright

To hear it go bong,
Clatter, giggle and beep,
So you shut your eyes tight,
Try to go back to sleep.

But when the alarm goes
At seven o'clock,
The house's mad antics
Suddenly stop!

And you wonder a while –
Is the house all it seems?
All those weird goings-on!
Or were they just dreams?

James Kirkup

13

Ghostly Lessons

Mum, I want some chocolate,
just one little treat –
peppermint or strawberry cream . . .

GHOSTS DON'T EAT!

Mum, I've got a toothache,
a pain beneath my heel;
my throat's too sore to work tonight. . .

GHOSTS DON'T FEEL!

Mum, I really hate the dark –
I hate the way they stared!
I'm scared of graveyards, woods and folk . . .

GHOSTS AREN'T SCARED!

Judith Nicholls

Who's Afraid?

Do I have to go haunting tonight?
The children might give me a fright.
It's dark in that house.
I might meet a mouse.
Do I have to go haunting tonight?

I don't like the way they scream out,
When they see me drifting about.
I'd much rather stay here,
Where there's nothing to fear.
Do I have to go haunting tonight?

John Foster

15

The Boastful Ghost

The boastful ghost flapped through a wall,
His white face full of glee,
'I'm much the bravest ghost there is,
A real ghoul,' said he,
'All living creatures great and small
Are terrified of me.'

Just then a bustling, bright-eyed mouse
Came hopping down the stair,
The ghost looked round, shrieked: 'Help!' and flew
To tremble on a chair,
And, passing by, the tiny mouse
Was heard to squeak: 'Oh yeah?'

Richard Edwards